Bb Tenor Saxophone
Volume 2

SAXOPHONE SOLOS
Bb Tenor with piano accompaniment
Editor: Paul Harvey

INDEX

CHESTER MUSIC

(A division of Music Sales Limited)
8/9 Frith Street, London W1V 5TZ

Z6-95

1
Bolero

p 1st time
mf 2nd time

2
Andante and Rondo

Haydn Millars

8

Rondo

For Dr. G.A. Low-Beer

3
Christopher's Calypso

Dorothy Harvey

4
Three Sketches from Bala
(i) Bala Breeze

Colin E. Cowles

(ii) Bala Ballade

18

(iii) Bala Bounce

5
Rue Maurice-Berteaux

Paul Harvey

6
Arioso

Printed and bound in Great Britain by
Caligraving Limited Thetford Norfolk

11/94 (19934)

EDITOR'S NOTES

1.   Bolero   Maurice Ravel (1875-1937)

The passage contained in bars 23 to 39 is the best known and most important of all orchestral tenor saxophone solos. The soprano saxophone solo consists of exactly the same notes.

2.   Andante and Rondo   Haydn Millars

This entertaining bassoon solo was discovered and adapted for the tenor saxophone by Maxwell Holgate. The composers's dates are unknown but he was probably Victorian.

3.   Christopher's Calypso   Dorothy Harvey

A rhythmic companion piece to "Christopher's Caper" in Volume 1.

4.   Three Scetches from Bala   Colin Cowles
    (i)   Bala Breeze
    (ii)   Bala Ballade
    (iii) Bala Bounce

These short pieces were composed by Bala Lake, North Wales in August 1977.

5.   Rue Maurice-Berteaux   Paul Harvey

The title refers to a street in Mantes La Ville, near Paris, where two of the world's leading saxophone manufacturer's have their factories. The piece suggests a typically bustling French street scene, with the sound of saxophones being tested inside the factories.

6.   Arioso   J. H. Fiocco (1703-1714)

One of the many Baroque oboe solos which are very suitable for the saxophone.

Paul Harvey, 1979.

SOUNDS FOR SAX

PIECES FOR
E♭ ALTO OR B♭ TENOR SAXOPHONE
AND PIANO

1 Carol Barratt/Karl Jenkins

1. RAZMATAZ RAG
2. JAZZ SOLO
3. BILL'S BOOGIE
4. TIME TO TANGO
5. LAZY HAZE
6. WALTZ IN BLUE

2 Richard Pepper

1. BLUE MARCH
2. ANGLO SAXON
3. PRIMITIVE BLUES

Parts are included for both
E♭ Alto and B♭ Tenor Saxophone

CHESTER MUSIC
(A division of Music Sales Ltd)
8/9 Frith Street, London W1V 5TZ

Flute   Editor: Trevor Wye

Oboe   Editor: James Brown

Clarinet   Editor: Thea King

Bassoon   Editor: William Waterhouse

Saxophone   Editor: Paul Harvey

A growing collection of volumes from Chester Music, containing a
wide range of pieces from different periods.

E♭ ALTO SAXOPHONE VOLUME I

Bizet	L'Arlesienne
Mussorgsky	The Old Castle
	from "Pictures at an Exhibition"
Delibes	Barcarolle
	from "Sylvia"
Kodaly	The Battle and Defeat of Napoleon
	from "Hary Janos"
Greaves	What is Beauty but a Breath?
Byrd	Pavane for the Earl of Salisbury
D. Harvey	Lullaby for a Saxophone
C. Blyton	In Memoriam Scott Fitzgerald

E♭ ALTO SAXOPHONE VOLUME II

Vaughan Williams	Dance of Job's Comforters
Sullivan	"The Sun and I"
J. S. Bach	Menuet
J. S. Bach	Badinerie
Handel	Allegro
D. Harvey	London's Burning
C. Cowles	Tolmers Village
P. Harvey	Caprice Anglais

B♭ TENOR SAXOPHONE VOLUME I

Welsh Trad.	The Red Piper's Melody
Saint-Saens	The Swan
Handel	Allegro from Suite XIV
Granados	Andaluza
Handel	"Love in Her Eyes Sits Playing"
D. Harvey	Christopher's Caper
C. Blyton	Saxe Blue
C. Blyton	Mock Joplin

B♭ TENOR SAXOPHONE VOLUME II

Ravel	Bolero
H. Millars	Andante and Rondo
D. Harvey	Christopher's Calypso
C. Cowles	Three Sketches from Bala
P. Harvey	Rue Maurice-Berteaux
Fiocco	Arioso

Also available: SAXOPHONE QUARTETS

Further details on request

CHESTER MUSIC
A division of Music Sales Ltd.
8/9 Frith Street, London, W1V 5TZ

Bb Tenor Saxophone
Volume 2

SAXOPHONE SOLOS
Bb Tenor with piano accompaniment
Editor: Paul Harvey

INDEX

CHESTER MUSIC

(A division of Music Sales Limited)
8/9 Frith Street, London W1V 5TZ

1
Bolero

Ravel

2
Andante and Rondo
Andante

Haydn Millars

Attacca Rondo

Rondo

For Dr. G.A. Low-Beer

3
Christopher's Calypso

Dorothy Harvey

4
Three Sketches from Bala
(i) Bala Breeze

(ii) Bala Ballade

(iii) Bala Bounce

Colin E. Cowles

5
Rue Maurice-Berteaux

Paul Harvey

6
Arioso

Fiocco